Brown Poetry

The Poetry of

Jamal Smith

ISBN: 978-1-71675-766-2

Intro

This edition combines the poems from the books *I Can't Breathe* and *To White People*. I wrote both of those books after seeing the tragic death of George Floyd. Shortly after, Breonna Taylor was senselessly murdered in her own home. I am tired of seeing trendy calls for change only after a brown person is murdered by the police, and….then nothing. I want change. I want meaningful change.

Brown Poetry

~~white people~~ be out there

praising a fictional foe

      Thanos—

His respite for resource distribution

Through quote-unquote

non-discriminatory genocide

and the death of billions

like some tested political theory

~~white people~~

are wild for pop culture

preposterousness

but talk about real slavery

      systematic genocide

      culture decimation still

happening to the African-American

in actual history

<u>Brown Poetry</u>

2

and they crumble

babbling *notallofus…*

attempting to seal up

their fragility

Brown Poetry

murderer George Zimmerman

became an artist

and sold THE GUN—

claiming it as historical

for an extensive amount

of money

There will be brightness

Derek Chauvin

sadly but true

this is what happens

Maybe Dancing With The Stars

A book deal maybe

with JUSTICE a distance thought

only to crop its needed face

<u>Brown Poetry</u>

4

the next time a minority

is murdered

Brown Poetry

Floyd's breath

can't help

Blow the

Black Lives Matter

Flag

Anymore

Nor

Utter those three

powerful words

Brown Poetry

6

Floyd cried

out for his Momma

words not lost in a lonely

      vacuum

but heard deeply by

every **black mother**

Brown Poetry

Why did it take another death

For ~~white people~~ to pretend

To be Allies again?

I see the memes

which are about as useful

as the third sleeve of a

knitted sweater for

a dead snake

Brown Poetry

ANTIFA and their rich

middle class whiteness

stole our protests for

their own political gain

no better than the politician

who care more for the

camera eye

than the racism **blacks**

see

Brown Poetry

Words are powerful. Throughout my life, there have been some phrases that have directly preceded riots.

"Why can't we all just get along?"

"Superior Court of California, County of Los Angeles; in the matter of the People of the State of California vs. Orenthal James Simpson, case number BA097211. We the jury in the above entitled action find the defendant Orenthal James Simpson not guilty..."

"These a**holes always get away."

"I can't breath."

Brown Poetry

When we learn about

looting private businesses

in response to

government cruelty,

the Boston Tea Party

has been shown

to students as an example

but looting Target is

a riot and horrible

both serve a purpose

why do we look at one

more favorably than the other?

Then ~~white people~~

come in and find every way

to tell us how it is different

how one was good and one was

Brown Poetry

11

bad

Brown Poetry

12

Not all ~~white people~~

They love to shout

While racist thoughts

Form into words

in their minds

Words that are alive

Damn right.

Said the Words.

Yes. All ~~white people~~.

Brown Poetry

13

How did Police Worship

Become the white reaction

to Black Lives Matters?

Is it easier to worship

the State and those in Blue

than face the inherent racism

inside of you?

~~white people~~ idolize the

State enforcers that are the source

of complaints and hatred

every other moment

other than the hot time after

a minority shooting?

<u>Brown Poetry</u>

14

The future should be in

the Cross

but ~~white people~~ have

put the Cross on its side

Brown Poetry

15

cutting off one arm

and now they have a billy club

and they worship the

State and the Blue

Praise the boys in blue

~~white people~~ chant

<u>Brown Poetry</u>

Brown Poetry

~~white people~~ are

Destroying their churches:

Starbucks, Chick-Fil-A,

And Target.

Their places of hope and refuge

with the hope that they

can end the racism they

have always been causing

but their white fragility

shatters much easier

than the window of

green logo spread-eagle

mermaid

<u>Brown Poetry</u>

18

I write poetry when I ache

in pain, the words flow furiously

There is no lack of

pain these days

Brown Poetry

19

Brown Poetry

Now we watch the politicians

reach for the spotlight

aim for attention

off the backs of Floyd

and **Black** protesters

cutting up their backs

with their shoes

like the whips off plantations

Brown Poetry

Jesus needs to come back

Quickly come back

with all his Arabic glory

and beautiful skin

to set the ~~white people~~

straight

<u>Brown Poetry</u>

22

Nothing I write is new

Nothing is deep

It's just like King

giving his speech:

boxed

and wrapped up

nice and neat

so ~~white people~~

can handle a powerful

black man

Brown Poetry

Dog eared pages, bent—folded—

For importance, for remembrance

Pen marks, crayon colors

Poking out verses

These are footsteps

On the perfect sands

Not corrupting, not changing

Always remaining despite

The tides of change

Brown Poetry

24

Why Are you here?

Rise Up

Go Home

<u>Brown Poetry</u>

This is us

for us

Brown Poetry

26

Was nothing learned

From the Scottsboro Boys?

History repeats

itself of course

1931

eighty-nine years

and **black people** are

still murdered

the blue are still worshiped

Brown Poetry

ENOUGH

It was already

ENOUGH

before the

plantations and

Middle Passage

ENOUGH

of trendy protests

only after a

murder

Brown Poetry

Legally litigating roles,

Races, ethnicities into equality

Is null for the litigated

Having the very power institution struggled against,

Yelled as the enemy,

Grant

Bestow

Gift the equality you desire?

Do you not see the issue?

The white establishment will litigate equality, not the
minorities themselves

Who really creates equality?

Who really institutes change?

Brown Poetry

29

You don't understand why riots need to happen

Brown Poetry

Black lives **DO** matter

Black lives could matter

Black likes should matter

But (non-deflecting)

Black lives don't matter

until there is a tragedy

then they matter for the

duration of the trendy protests

<u>Brown Poetry</u>

Why was I born this way, asked the slave?

Why was I born this way, asked the poor **black**?

Why was I born this way, asked the prison pipeline
student?

Do not pee at Jesus' feet

or persevere through an existential crisis

It is the ~~white man~~ who keeps us weak

Fight

protest

gather

educate

We the people

persevere and

don't pretend we

can change the world

through slacktivism

Brown Poetry

Maybe he shouldn't have

committed a crime

Did he have a record?

Did criminal record carrying Floyd deserve to die?

Brown Poetry

~~whites~~ yell

Go ahead, black lives matter! Why wait?

Burn down your own neighborhoods.

Destroy your own Section 8 housing.

Loot your own stores.

Shoot each other.

Bring an end to any future city planning in your neighborhoods.

Repeat history.

Repeat stupidity.

Brown Poetry

Awareness

donations

marching

throwing rocks

is not going to

destroy your

privilege ~~white man~~

memes and

slacktivism just

make you

look more horrible

Brown Poetry

35

Now watch

~~white people~~

read this book

and praise it as

the exotic Other book

Brown Poetry

36

You want me to
pull myself up by my
bootstraps
but you confuse
'me' with 'you'
and 'bootstraps'
with 'noose.'

Brown Poetry

Why do I need to

fight riot police and

smell tear gas

every time the news

catches onto

the death of a

black man?

Brown Poetry

38

Tweet about racism

Facebook it

Hang a sign in

your white window

Rename 'rioters'

You have done nothing—

No; less than nothing

Brown Poetry

Black lives matter

  lack (of understanding among   ~~whites~~)

      matter (not better and   not

only matter)

    lives (because we want to live)

Bla   m e (everything else   except

the main   problem)

Brown Poetry

Don't get offended

on my behalf

fuck fuck fuck you

make a change

cause calamity

in your heart

about your own RACISM

spread the severity

of the situation surrounding

us

from the individual

to the neighborhood

to the community

to the state

Brown Poetry

Eight minutes forty-six seconds Black Lives Matter Black
Lives Matter Black Lives Matter Black Lives Matter Black
Lives Matter Black Lives Matter Black Lives Matter Black
Lives Matter Black Lives Matter Black Lives Matter Black
Lives Matter Black Lives Matter Black Lives Matter Black
Lives Matter Black Lives Matter Black Lives Matter Black
Lives Matter Black Lives Matter Black Lives Matter Black
Lives Matter Black Lives Matter Black Lives Matter Black
Lives Matter Black Lives Matter Black Lives Matter Black
Lives Matter Black Lives Matter Black Lives Matter Black
Lives Matter Black Lives Matter Black Lives Matter Black
Lives Matter Black Lives Matter Black Lives Matter Black
Lives Matter Black Lives Matter Black Lives Matter Black
Lives Matter Black Lives Matter Black Lives Matter Black
Lives Matter Black Lives Matter Black Lives Matter Black
Lives Matter Black Lives Matter Black Lives Matter Black
Lives Matter Black Lives Matter Black Lives Matter Black
Lives Matter Black Lives Matter Black Lives Matter Black
Lives Matter Black Lives Matter Black Lives Matter Black
Lives Matter Black Lives Matter Black Lives Matter Black
Lives Matter Black Lives Matter Black Lives Matter Black

<u>Brown Poetry</u>

42

Lives Matter Black Lives Matter Black Lives Matter Black
Lives Matter Black Lives Matter Black Lives Matter Black
Lives Matter Black Lives Matter Black Lives Matter Black
Lives Matter Black Lives Matter Black Lives Matter Black
Lives Matter Black Lives Matter Black Lives Matter Black
Lives Matter Black Lives Matter Black Lives Matter Black
Lives Matter Black Lives Matter Black Lives Matter Black
Lives Matter Black Lives Matter Black Lives Matter Black
Lives Matter Black Lives Matter Black Lives Matter Black
Lives Matter Black Lives Matter Black Lives Matter Black
Lives Matter Black Lives Matter Black Lives Matter Black
Lives Matter Black Lives Matter Black Lives Matter Black
Lives Matter Black Lives Matter Black Lives Matter Black
Lives Matter Black Lives Matter Black Lives Matter Black
Lives Matter Black Lives Matter Black Lives Matter Black
Lives Matter Black Lives Matter Black Lives Matter Black
Lives Matter Black Lives Matter Black Lives Matter Black
Lives Matter Black Lives Matter Black Lives Matter Black
Lives Matter Black Lives Matter Black Lives Matter Black
Lives Matter Black Lives Matter Black Lives Matter Black
Lives Matter Black Lives Matter Black Lives Matter

<u>Brown Poetry</u>

43

The amount of time it took you to read those four pages is
the time a knee was crushing George Floyd's neck

Brown Poetry

Brown Poetry

45

No words on that page

No justice for Floyd

No justice for many

Brown Poetry

46

history has shown

the more we fight

the higher the

chances we end

up under the boot

Brown Poetry

I'm not a writer

I'm a pen and paper owner

I yield to those

whose words have

pierced the racial problem

I just use dead white man

style to portray elementary

thoughts that should be known.

Brown Poetry

There's a hell of a change
to be made out there
go
fight

Brown Poetry

REGISTER OF ACTIONS
CASE NO. 27-CR-20-12646

State of Minnesota vs Derek Michael Chauvin		
§	Case Type:	Crim/Traf Mandatory
§	Date Filed:	05/29/2020
§ § §	Location:	Hennepin Criminal/Traffic/ Petty Downtown

PARTY INFORMATION

			Lead Attorneys
Defendant	Chauvin, Derek Michael Oakdale, MN 55128	Male DOB: 03/19/1976	~~MATTHEW GLEN FRANK~~ *Retained* 651-757-1448~~(W)~~
Jurisdiction	State of Minnesota		MATTHEW GLEN FRANK 651-757-1448(W)

CASE INFORMATION

Charges: Chauvin, Derek Michael	Statute	Level	Date	Disposition	Level of Sentence

Ah, this is not justice

Rather, recommended reading

A wish to stop the rampant Nile

<u>Brown Poetry</u>

Among the blue bullets

Brown Poetry

'cause comfort comes

from the furious

salad tossing

Chauvin & Thoa

Lane & Kueng

will do in

Oak Park Heights

Brown Poetry

Yes Chauvin

it's hard to breath

and cry MOMMA

with your tongue

in an inmate's used ectum

Brown Poetry

in prison

Knee in the neck

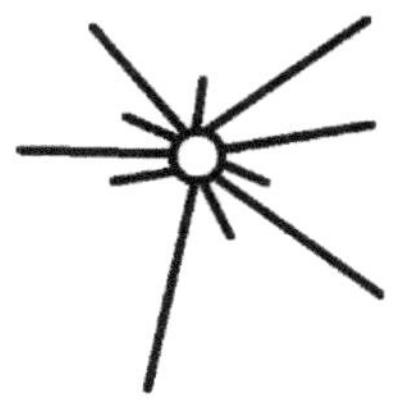

Leads to a tongue in a

prisoner's ass

Brown Poetry

it's not justice

it's just pleasant

Brown Poetry

I see white people

putting on self made

hero capes

with minority slogans

(*to makes themselves feel*

happy)

they share memes

jump to virtual signal

& the often slacktivism

has created a whole

new world where

white people are still

the Saviors of all

<u>Brown Poetry</u>

Black Lives Matter

three words

sixteen letters

and white people

steal them

and rewrite them

claiming them

<u>Brown Poetry</u>

Black Lives Matter

Is yelled, chanted, written,

     graffitied, branded, tattooed

Black. Lives. Matter.

But, you hear:

ONLY Black Live Matter

White Lives Don't Matter

Back People Are Better

Kill All White People

Black Power

Kill Whitey

It's just three words

and you hear WHITE

Brown Poetry

ANTIFA

you ain't black

ANTIFA

you ain't helping

ANTIFA

stay in your middle-class homes

in your white neighborhoods

and buy your designer

Antifa costumes

with your trust funds

ANTIFA

I don't need

your agreement

pity and support

Brown Poetry

white people,

it is extremely difficult to

be told you didn't work

as hard as you thought

culture held your hand

it's not about you, white people

not everything is about you

everything has been on your side

everything since the beginning

have aided you

you worked hard, yes

but it's not just you

this is hard to hear

I know

Brown Poetry

it's hard to still have

a foot on the plantation

Brown Poetry

I too sing America

the red white & blue

the Constitution is paper

society if volatile

I too sing America

as I hopefully stare at a

non-racist country

(*it is only a fictional painting*)

Brown Poetry

white people

you unhelpfully flipped

over police cars and

spray painted BLM

you yelled and burned

you flexed

and got your wish

to stand next to sin

<u>Brown Poetry</u>

Alright, Ralph…

I mean, white people

(*squeaky voice*)

"I'm helping."

Brown Poetry

Blues lives matter…

now a job of the state

is equal to a race?

Beautiful skin and a rich history

equivalent to a profession?

This is your reaction to BLM,

white people?

<u>Brown Poetry</u>

As a law enforcement officer I solemnly swear to uphold the constitution of the United States and of the State of Minnesota;

That I will bear true faith and allegiance to the same;

That I will enforce the laws of the United States, of the State of Minnesota, and of the City of Saint Paul impartially;

That I will work in partnership with the public of the City of Saint Paul toward providing a safe environment and enhancing the quality of life consistent with the values of our community;

That I will adhere to the ethical values of professionalism, integrity, responsiveness, sensitivity, respect and openness;

That I take this obligation freely, without any mental reservation or purpose of evasion; and that I will well and faithfully discharge the duties of the office on which I am about to enter. So help me God.

Brown Poetry

I wish I had something more to say about this actual oath

Jesus died for all

but not all lives matter

here, to us

equality is still

a discussion

often an argument

Brown Poetry

Two poetic words (*to you*)

Fuck You.

Brown Poetry

George Floyd had

drugs in the system

poor health

was drunk

didn't deserve a

knee to the neck

Brown Poetry

Our crime stories

usually end with gunshots

death & a finale to a forcefully

downtrodden life

not with

executive producer Dick Wolf

Brown Poetry

a knee on a football field

that brought more knees

shattered more white

fragility then Chauvin's

knee brought outrage

Brown Poetry

Stop with the white guilt

I don't need you to feel guilty

and see you post on your iphone

you will blur the issue

in whiteness

and cloth it in white

as your wait outside the Panera

for the scary part of the protest

to end

Brown Poetry

JUSTICE
|
|
|
I am white
this is about me

Brown Poetry

Racist

    Racist

        Racist

            Racist

                Nazi

                    Nazi

How many times will you say these?

You've already said them so

many times for anything

and everything, the words

have lost their meanings

and power

you stole these words to

Brown Poetry

use for anyone who

disagrees with you

racism can't afford to

be degraded

Brown Poetry

Racism is a vile virus

that's gone viral

with accessible video

Brown Poetry

Nelson Mandela lifted our Spirits

Tiger Woods caught our eyes

Obama had our hearts

Black Panther raises up the youth

they need a hero

Brown Poetry

I too sing America

I sing in the classroom

    as a teacher

I sing it to lift pride

Brown Poetry

Black and white

Black and white

You just shut the blinds to racism out there

We are Kunta Kinte

We can't run away

We can't escape racism

systematic & overt

Brown Poetry

I am still caged

Among this Mormon landscape

and love for Christ

I am still caged

In this desert

among the Temples

I am still caged

but I don't need your sympathy

or guilt or your white feelings

I am still caged

This is just daily life

Brown Poetry

We real cool. We
ain't scared no more. We
punch racists. We
fight them. We
bring change.

We get pushed aside. We
are below the blue. We
get shot soon.

Brown Poetry

Can't fight what you can't see?

We see racism everywhere

Can't fight what you can't see?

You'll crack a clear window

and reduce racism to a Tweet

Can't fight what you can't see?

Racism is still out there and seen

Brown Poetry

Only when George Floyd

wanted to breath

cried for Momma

did you break your silence

a silence deep as an abyss

since Ferguson and

Michael Brown

and before that

deep silence following

Trayvon Martin

buying skittles and tea

Imagine them wearing black

Imagine until you see

everything in black

'cause you ain't gonna

see anything from black

as black and through black

Brown Poetry

Jesus

reaches

out

Brown Poetry

Epstein didn't kill himself

COVID-19 is real

Arrest the officers who killed

Breonna Taylor

Brown Poetry

www.ingramcontent.com/pod-product-compliance
Lightning Source LLC
Chambersburg PA
CBHW061510250726
48657CB00005B/1780